MW01181381

*Between the humble and contrite heart
and the majesty of heaven, there are no barriers;
the only password is prayer.*

HOSEA BALLOU

Requests for information should be addressed to:
Inspirio, the gift group of Zondervan
Grand Rapids, Michigan 49530
www.inspiriogifts.com

Compilers: Rebecca Currington, Christy Philippe, and Betsy Williams in
    conjunction with SnapdragonGroup^SM Editorial Services
Project Manager: Kim Zeilstra
Design Manager: Michael J. Williams
Production Manager: Matt Nolan
Design: Brand Navigation, www.brandnavigation.com
Cover image: istockphoto.com, Anna Chelnokova

Printed in China
07 08 09 / 4 3 2 1

The GIFT of PRAYER

INSPIRATIONAL STORIES
of GOD'S WORK

inspirio®

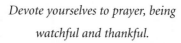

Devote yourselves to prayer, being
watchful and thankful.

COLOSSIANS 4:2

CONTENTS

INTRODUCTION

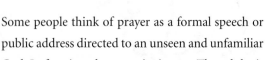

Some people think of prayer as a formal speech or public address directed to an unseen and unfamiliar God. In fact, just the opposite is true. Though he is unseen, he need not be unfamiliar. We can know him — personally — and prayer is how we do that.

The Bible describes prayer as conversation, communication, a normal expression of relationship between a personal God and those he has created in his image. We are urged to call on Him frequently and with the confidence of a beloved child seeking out a doting father. Though he is to be respected and honored, he is also accessible and interested in our plight.

Within the pages of this book, *The Gift of Prayer*, we have worked to illuminate the nature and characteristics of prayer, both through biblical accounts and stories of prayer experienced by everyday people just like you. We hope that as you read, you will see prayer as an essential element of the Christian experience and a priceless gift from a loving Father.

BIBLICAL TRUTHS ABOUT PRAYER

⌒

- Prayer is a gift from God, generously given, without consideration of our worthiness or our unworthiness. Sinners as well as saints can pray.

- Prayer is simple conversation with almighty God, made possible by the mediation of one man—God's Son, Jesus Christ.

- Prayer comes from the heart, sometimes expressed in words and other times a wordless cry from deep within.

- Prayer is fed by faith, believing that God hears and will answer.

- Prayer should be steady and unwavering—even when no answer is in sight—acknowledging that God answers prayer according to his own will and purpose and in his own perfect timing.

Prayers for God's Intervention

———— ∞ ————

Deal with your servant according to your love.

It is time for you to act, O LORD.

PSALM 119:124, 126

———— ∞ ————

---

*Soften up, G*OD*, and intervene;*

hurry and get me some help.

PSALM 40:13 MSG

Never make the blunder of trying to forecast the way

God is going to answer your prayer.

OSWALD CHAMBERS

PRAYERS FOR GOD'S INTERVENTION

DEFEATING THE FIERCE WARRIORS

My husband and I weren't new to child rearing. We had successfully raised five children—two girls and three boys. The teen years were stressful, but we had applauded as each one came through the adolescent fog seemingly unscathed, declared independence, and went on to lead normal, happy lives—give or take a minor speed bump from time to time. Perhaps we had even been a little smug. We thought we had made it through the danger years. We could not have imagined that we would see our middle son—a loving husband and father, a high achiever, and a funny, engaging person with great style and charm—enslaved to drugs.

Of course there were little warning signs along the way. Changes in his physical appearance, loss of weight, and a general restlessness. An unusual talkativeness with less and less cogency. There were whispers that he was having issues at work and at home, but we explained them away. We knew our

PRAYERS FOR GOD'S INTERVENTION

son. None of this could possibly be true.

But gradually, the signs became too obvious to ignore.

On Thanksgiving Day, our family's biggest holiday, Greg stayed outside all day. Uncharacteristically sullen and noncommunicative, he came in only to eat and then told everyone he was working on the radio in his truck.

On Christmas Day, as soon as dinner was over, he lay down on the floor and slept for almost eight hours. His weight dropped so drastically that it was painful to see him. And his wife told us that he was rarely home, spending almost all his time at a rental house he had purchased across town.

At this point, we had been praying for a while. Greg's father, his wife, his grandparents, and his sisters and brothers were all on board. We made calls to many people who knew and loved our son, and they agreed to pray as well.

We looked at the options. An "intervention" (where friends and family members meet to con-

PRAYERS FOR GOD'S INTERVENTION

front an addicted person) was considered as a possibility. We had seen these on television and thought perhaps our family—if we could come together as a loving, united force—might be able to convince him to accept help and receive treatment. But counselors told us these also had a poor rate of sucess—less than 10 percent.

We tried talking. Each of us made an attempt to get through to Greg with reason and logic. None of us were able to even break the first barrier. He assured us he did not have a problem.

Everything—up to and including his physical life—was at stake. His marriage, his relationship with his children, his job, his finances, his home, nothing escaped the black, odious vapor that is drug addiction.

This was the situation in which we found ourselves on the day the email came. A coworker suggested that we read a passage from the book of Isaiah. These are the words of hope we found there: "Can plunder be taken from warriors, or captives

PRAYERS FOR GOD'S INTERVENTION

rescued from the fierce? This is what the LORD says: "Yes, captives will be taken from warriors, and plunder retrieved from the fierce; I will contend with those who contend with you, and your children I will save" (Isaiah 49:24–25).

Those words came alive in our hearts and our minds. New hope encouraged us to enter into battle. The Lord was fighting with us. We could not lose. We were not capable of delivering our precious son from the "fierce warrior" called drugs. But God was!

In the months ahead, we feasted on prayer as the battle raged.

When deliverance came, it looked a lot like jail. When the police searched the rental house, they uncovered only a pipe, some money, and a "half-a-dime" bag of methamphetamines—but it was enough. Eighty pounds lighter, wearing just one shoe, and barely aware of his surroundings, our son was put into the police car.

The next week was the most difficult any of us could remember. We agreed as a family that we

PRAYERS FOR GOD'S INTERVENTION

could not respond to Greg's pleas to get him out of jail until the drugs had loosened their death grip on his mind. We prayed together in groups and alone, through the day and the nighttime hours. His frantic phone calls came every few hours, pleading with us to come for him. God kept us strong through prayer.

Four days after his arrest, we saw him coming back to his right mind. Finally, he agreed to go into treatment. Though there was much work still to be done, we knew the battle had turned in our favor.

This week our family and friends will celebrate the one-year anniversary of Greg's victory over drugs. The date is marked from the day of his one and only relapse, a week after he finished treatment. The rental house is long gone. The long work hours are also gone. The so-called friends who sanctioned and abetted his drug use are gone as well. God has restored his marriage and given him a whole new life. Though our son was headed for a terrible fate, God intervened—threw up a roadblock that

PRAYERS FOR GOD'S INTERVENTION

kept him from being swept off that cliff into the blackness below.

We know there are battles yet to come. But we aren't afraid. Through prayer we will defeat our enemy's fierce warriors whenever and wherever we encounter them.[1]

In my distress I called to the LORD;
I cried to my God for help.
From his temple he heard my voice;
my cry came before him, into his ears.

PSALM 18:6

That the Almighty does make use of human agencies
and directly intervenes in human affairs is one of the
plainest statements in the Bible.

ABRAHAM LINCOLN

PRAYERS FOR GOD'S INTERVENTION

WHOOSH!

Do you think God answers only those prayers prefaced with "thee" or "thou"? Do you believe that anything else would be blasphemous, or at the very least, a waste of his precious time? That's what I believed ... until the day I discovered what mattered to me was important to God.

My husband and I were only three years into our marriage and living with cat hair, dog hair, and a dark brown, threadbare carpet that showed all the dust, crumbs, and spills that happened at our house. And now Scotty had called to say he'd be bringing home out-of-town colleagues *and* his boss!

"You can't be serious!" I said. "The house is a *mess*!" I had nothing to cook—or wear! "And the carpet?" I checked the heavy breathing about to become a burst of airy panic. "*I can't* entertain—"

"Babe ..." He wasn't insisting, but I knew he needed me to do this. I pictured my husband's grin and imagined how proud he'd be showing off his home.

PRAYERS FOR GOD'S INTERVENTION

"Okay," I said, hoping I sounded cheerful. There weren't that many hours, but I'd be ready.

Hanging up, though, my courage evaporated! First, I'd need to make a run to the store and then clean every room. I would load "Moonlight Sonata" into the stereo and disguise all my clutter and dust. Then I would shower and make myself presentable. I would also bake a cake and toss a terrific salad. I would toss the dog and cat too! Our teen, who spilled books, clothing, and cola from one end of the house to the other, would need a more personal arrangement.

With the house nearly company-ready and my wet head wrapped in my husband's oldest robe, I found my prettiest dishes, cut flowers, and polished everything except our daughter's den.

It took three hours to get my act almost together. I was down to changing from Scotty's robe to my own clothing and dragging out the vacuum. If I could just get the crumbs, hairs, and any other disgusting debris—"Then I'll get dressed and hooray!"

PRAYERS FOR GOD'S INTERVENTION

Jerking the vacuum out of the front hall closet, I tucked Scotty's robe snug around my queasy middle. Our canister cleaner wasn't exactly wonderful, but it had never let me down, even though I'd worked it harder than the instructions had recommended.

Rounding the first corner, I yanked the frayed cord, flipped the switch, and began pushing the brushes back and forth over threads and the remains of a cupcake—it sputtered, coughed, and then there was nothing.

"No! Not now!" I said, "Not with guests only minutes from dinner and me in Scotty's chenille—"

On my knees, I shook the hose, grabbed it around what felt like its throat, pinched the plug to shove it deeper into the outlet, and flipped the switch a second and third time. That close to the floor, the litter and mess looked even worse! In exactly sixteen minutes, they would all be coming! "*Please*," I pleaded, shaking the entire machine and

PRAYERS FOR GOD'S INTERVENTION

grabbing a fork from the table, thinking there might be something stuck that could be fished out.

Only there wasn't, so I began shaking it like a dog with a slipper, shouting if it wouldn't work it would be going to the dump! I glanced at the clock. In exactly fifteen minutes, my husband would come through our front door and I'd be in his ratty robe with my hair in sweaty ringlets and with our house still looking like a total disaster!

On my knees, I threw my hands into the air shouting, "Can't YOU help?"

What I heard next was not God's still small voice, nor angel's wings. There was simply a "*Whoosh*!"—as hairs, crumbs, and whatever else had clogged that weary hose came loose. "Whoosh!" With goose bumps, I watched an ugly carpet become something almost lovely. With only seconds to spare, I checked hot dishes, changed from Scotty's robe to something hopefully becoming, and greeted my husband's smile with one of my own.

Within minutes, I was also meeting Scotty's

PRAYERS FOR GOD'S INTERVENTION

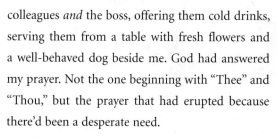

colleagues *and* the boss, offering them cold drinks, serving them from a table with fresh flowers and a well-behaved dog beside me. God had answered my prayer. Not the one beginning with "Thee" and "Thou," but the prayer that had erupted because there'd been a desperate need.

Today, I pray occasionally in a supermarket, often in the car dashing to where I don't want to be, or doing a chore I think I can't handle. I simply lift my heart, thoughts, and voice to the God who loves me — the same God who invited me to come to him with any need, because nothing is too difficult or too unimportant for him. Everything that matters to me also matters to my Creator.

He's near to *all* who call on him. He even created us to be a little lower than the angels … low enough to cry out on our knees … even when the "enemy" is only a vacuum cleaner.[2]

PRAYERS FOR GOD'S INTERVENTION

God knows how often I pray for you. Day and night I bring you and your needs in prayer to the one I serve with all my might.

ROMANS 1:9 TLB

Talking to men for God is a great thing, but talking to God for men is greater still.

EDWARD MCKENDREE BOUNDS

PRAYERS FOR GOD'S INTERVENTION

COULD THIS BE THE SOMETHING?

My husband, Jobey, and I were on the ropes. We were barely speaking to one another, and our voices were usually raised when we did. Our financial situation was the biggest stressor — too little money and too much month. Our son, Connor, was just starting kindergarten, and it would be at least a year before he went to school all day, and then I could get a full-time job. We should have been able to work past the money issues, but the bills crept into every aspect of our relationship — robbing us of our joy and our love for each other.

We did try. Jobey and I planned romantic date nights — but they usually ended in fights over how much we were spending. We sat down for long conversations, each suggesting compromises we could make to ease our financial ills. But in the end, we each had our own point of view and neither was willing to compromise. Eventually, our biggest topic of conversation was our impending separation.

PRAYERS FOR GOD'S INTERVENTION

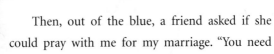

Then, out of the blue, a friend asked if she could pray with me for my marriage. "You need some divine intervention," she said. It was a concept I had not even considered.

When we first began to pray together, things actually seemed to get worse at home. But my friend said that we must keep praying. "The enemy just doesn't want to let go, so he's fighting your prayers," she told me. "Don't worry," she added. "God never loses a fight!"

Then one day while doing something as mundane as cleaning our bathroom, I sank to my knees and sensed the Lord urging me to pray. It was a simple prayer, "Lord, my friend and I have been praying, but the situation seems to be getting worse instead of better. If it is in your will for us to stay together, then please do something that will turn the tide and restore our broken relationship. If your plans are for us to be apart, please give me the strength to carry on without him. Either way, I now put my trust completely in you for you alone can

PRAYERS FOR GOD'S INTERVENTION

make things right."

Before I could even get to my feet, I knew the answer and wondered why I hadn't known it before. Perhaps in my stubborn heart, I had refused to even entertain the possibility. Now, suddenly, it seems perfectly obvious—the touch of nausea in the morning, an unusual tiredness, and that one other symptom that could not be dismissed. Could this be the "something" I had asked God for, his way of bringing my husband and me back together?

The next day, a pregnancy test confirmed it. Jobey and I were going to have a baby. For a while panic plagued my heart. What if my husband still wasn't interested in making our marriage work? But God quickly reminded me that I had placed my marriage in his hands. Slowly but surely, my heart became peaceful.

It may sound strange, even faithless, but I couldn't find the courage to tell Jobey in person. Instead I called him at work and just blurted out the news. He didn't say much, and we hung up

PRAYERS FOR GOD'S INTERVENTION

rather quickly.

Jobey came home early that evening and wrapped his arms around me. That night, after putting Connor to bed, we sat on the couch in each other's arms. We didn't speak about my pregnancy until the next morning after dropping Connor off at school. We had told him that he was going to be a big brother, and his excitement was so pure, so ecstatic.

That morning, I told Jobey about my friend and how she had agreed to pray with me that our marriage would be healed. He listened carefully. Then we prayed together, the two of us, hand in hand before God.

Over the next few months, we discussed how much the pregnancy made us realize all that we would have lost if we had chosen to get a divorce. Our budget was, and still is, tight. But our attitudes are not. We take all our worries and lay them at God's feet. He intervened once—we knew he would do it again.

PRAYERS FOR GOD'S INTERVENTION

As I sit here now, typing with one hand and rocking my little girl to sleep, I continue to thank God every day for this precious treasure — God's perfect plan of hope and healing — our little Savannah.[3]

PRAYERS FOR GOD'S
INTERVENTION

Pray? Why pray?

What can praying do?

Praying really changes things, arranges life anew.

It's good for your digestion, gives

peaceful sleep at night

And fills the grayest, gloomiest day—

with rays of glowing light.

HELEN STEINER RICE

PRAYERS FOR GOD'S INTERVENTION

MOTHER LECTURE NUMBER SEVEN

"Honey, what about Mother Lecture Number Seven?" For many years that's all I needed to say. My grown son, Jim, would know this was my way of asking, "Have you started back to church yet?" He would squirm a bit as he replied, "Not yet, Mom, maybe next week." We both knew he would not be at church next week or the week after that.

I realize church attendance does not save a person, but I was certain it could be the first step for Jim someday renewing his relationship with the Lord. I desperately desired that for my son, even if he didn't want it for himself.

Jim had become a Christian when he was just eight years old. And he followed his decision with baptism. Growing up in a Christian home, his life included weekly doses of Sunday school and youth group activities. But like so many people, once he left home, he lived by his own guidelines, ceased

PRAYERS FOR GOD'S INTERVENTION

going to church, and ignored his relationship with Christ. I prayed for him each day, asking God to do whatever it took to bring him back into a relationship with him. I had no idea what that would be, and I wrestled with some of the unpleasant solutions God might employ to bring it about. Still, I had to let God work things out his way and in his timing.

Jim married and began a family. His wife was not a Christian, and from all outward appearances, their home did not reflect anything of Christ. In my daily devotions, I continually brought their names to the Father, reminding him that the Bible said to raise a child properly and when he was old he would not depart from those teachings. I thought I had done that. Years passed, and things were still the same. Many times I wondered how "old" is old. How old would he have to be before he would return to the Lord? My prayers for him became longer, more intense.

As the years rolled on, Jim's marriage had its

PRAYERS FOR GOD'S INTERVENTION

ups and downs, and he still had not remembered Mother Lecture Number Seven. I determined not to nag him, but I began fasting one day a week, begging God to restore my son's faith. I acknowledged to God that there were days when my faith was weak, but I was reminded of those verses in James that say, "Ask in faith with no doubting…." I purposed in my heart to keep trusting.

As I walked through my neighborhood each morning, I always brought Jim's name to the Father. I like the Scripture that says, "Ask and it will be given you, seek and you shall find, knock and it will be opened unto you." To me it meant to keep storming the gates of heaven for the answer that I sought. Praying and fasting is all I have known to do, so that's exactly what I have done—with tears streaming down my face.

Earlier this year, Jim's wife talked about a divorce and Jim seemed to have reached an all-time low. He was tired of being in an unhappy marriage, and he didn't like the man he saw in his mirror or

PRAYERS FOR GOD'S INTERVENTION

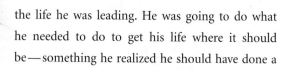

the life he was leading. He was going to do what he needed to do to get his life where it should be—something he realized he should have done a long time ago.

One Sunday morning, he ended up in a lovely church. He was amazed at the wonderful things he began to learn about God and just how good he felt talking to him once again. He continued going each week and soon rededicated his life to God, joined a Bible study, joined the church, and was rebaptized. He even stopped drinking and started losing weight.

Today he is becoming a new man inside and out, and it is a great joy to my heart to hear him quote Scripture and talk about the things God is showing him.

He wants his wife to attend church with him, and things are looking up for them. I am still praying about their relationship and that their marriage counseling will be helpful. But however things work out, Jim is determined that God will remain first in his life.

PRAYERS FOR GOD'S INTERVENTION

Now I know how "old" old is. For Jim, it was forty-five. He will never realize how many prayers were offered on his behalf or the tears I have shed for him, and that's all right. I take no credit for his returning to the Lord. That is a work only the Holy Spirit can do, but I will be forever delighted that Jim's first step back came because God prompted him to remember Mother Lecture Number Seven.[4]

PRAYERS FOR GOD'S INTERVENTION

Hear my prayer, O LORD,

listen to my cry for help.

PSALM 39:12

Never wait for fitter time or place to talk to him. To
wait till you go to church or to your room is to make
him wait. He will listen as you walk.

GEORGE MACDONALD

PRAYERS FOR GOD'S INTERVENTION

ALL'S RIGHT WITH THE WORLD

As they rode in a cab up Central Park West, the children were practically jumping out of their skin from excitement. They were on their way to the Museum of Natural History, a place filled with wonders. Coming into New York City was always a treat.

With their faces close to the windows, the children marveled at the size of the buildings and the number of people. As often as they came in to New York City from their home in New Jersey, the city never ceased to amaze them. They were glad that their aunt worked in the city and knew it so well.

Cristina had been looking forward to this excursion as much as her nephew, four-year-old Jamie, and her niece, Alexis, who was eight years old. New York City, with its park, its museums, its zoo, and everything else it has to offer, is a child's dream. This is especially true when you have an aunt who enjoys taking you there just as much as you love to go. Cristina truly loved these outings with the two

PRAYERS FOR GOD'S INTERVENTION

youngsters, because her son was a young adult now. She missed the joy of having a child with her to explore the city and now she had two.

"Were there dinosaurs when you were a little girl in Romania? Please, can we see the dinosaurs first, Tintin?" asked Jamie.

"No, no, the chocolate exhibit first. Please, please," cried her niece. "And then, Tintin, can we go to the planetarium?"

The young man driving the cab softly chuckled. Cristina laughed and giggled with Alexis and Jamie as they discussed their plans for the day.

At last they reached the museum. The driver pulled up to the curb. Cristina helped the children out of the cab and paid the young man, who called out, "Have fun at the museum, kids!" before he sped away down Central Park West. Jamie and Alexis, with their boundless energy, ran ahead.

The children waited impatiently for Tintin to catch up. She finally reached them, but as they were about to go through the revolving doors that

PRAYERS FOR GOD'S INTERVENTION

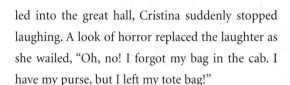

led into the great hall, Cristina suddenly stopped laughing. A look of horror replaced the laughter as she wailed, "Oh, no! I forgot my bag in the cab. I have my purse, but I left my tote bag!"

Both children froze in their tracks. Their aunt took each of them by the hand and started back down the stairs. Even at their young age, Jamie and Alexis appreciated the gravity of the situation, and so they quietly followed and didn't say a word. At the curb, Cristina stopped a cab that was passing by and asked the cab driver if there was a telephone number for the lost and found. The driver said, "Lady, you should have taken the receipt. There are dozens of garages, and you have to know which one to call. I hate to tell you this, but even if you knew which one it was, it isn't likely that you'll get your bag back." Realizing how upset she was, he added, "But maybe someone will turn it in to the police station. There's a precinct near here. Try them."

"Oh, children," their aunt cried. "I promise we will go to the museum, but first I want to go to the

PRAYERS FOR GOD'S INTERVENTION

police station. Perhaps somebody will bring my tote bag back. I can give them my name so they can call me if it turns up later on. There is nothing of value in it to anyone but me. But to me, my most precious possession was in there. You've seen it. It is my Bible. On the inside cover it says, 'To Mother, on her fortieth birthday. From your son, Mike.' A day doesn't pass without my reading it. I carry it with me everywhere I go.

Seeing how disappointed the children were at the prospect of leaving the museum, Cristina changed her mind. "You know what?" she said. "Let's go to the museum first. We can go to the police station later. That will give more time for someone to turn it in."

The trio sadly started back up the stairs and were about to enter the revolving doors to the museum for the second time. Feeling helpless, Cristina stopped a moment, closed her tear-filled eyes, and prayed, "Please, God, help me find my Bible."

PRAYERS FOR GOD'S INTERVENTION

Less than a minute after Christina opened her eyes, Alexis called out, "Tintin, look!"

There, on the park side of Central Park West across from the museum, a cab had pulled up to the curb and stopped. A tall, handsome man jumped out of the driver's seat. Without even taking the time to completely close the door of the cab, he ran across the street.

Cristina's mouth dropped as she recognized the cab driver. While Jamie and Alexis jumped up and down, their aunt began laughing and crying at the same time. The young man was smiling broadly as he raced up the stairs, two at a time, reached Cristina, and joyously handed her the gray tote bag. Her prayer had been answered, God had intervened. And her most precious possession, her Bible, had been restored to her.[5]

PRAYERS FOR GOD'S INTERVENTION

*Prayer is not something we do at a specific time,
but something we do all the time.*

RICHARD OWEN ROBERTS

*Be not far from me, O God;
come quickly, O my God, to help me.*

PSALM 71:12

PRAYERS FOR GOD'S INTERVENTION

ONE MAN'S PRAYER

When Adoni-zedek, the king of Jerusalem, heard how Joshua had captured and destroyed Ai and had killed its king, the same as he had done at Jericho, and how the people of Gibeon had made peace with Israel and were now their allies, he was very frightened. For Gibeon was a great city—as great as the royal cities and much larger than Ai—and its men were known as hard fighters. So King Adoni-zedek of Jerusalem sent messengers to several other kings: King Hoham of Hebron, King Piram of Jarmuth, King Japhia of Lachish, King Debir of Eglon.

"Come and help me destroy Gibeon," he urged them, "for they have made peace with Joshua and the people of Israel."

So these five Amorite kings combined their armies for a united attack on Gibeon. The men of Gibeon hurriedly sent messengers to Joshua at Gilgal.

PRAYERS FOR GOD'S INTERVENTION

"Come and help your servants!" they demanded. "Come quickly and save us! For all the kings
of the Amorites who live in the hills are here with
their armies."

So Joshua and the Israeli army left Gilgal and
went to rescue Gibeon.

"Don't be afraid of them," the Lord said to
Joshua, "for they are already defeated! I have given
them to you to destroy. Not a single one of them
will be able to stand up to you."

Joshua traveled all night from Gilgal and took
the enemy armies by surprise. Then the Lord threw
them into a panic so that the army of Israel slaugh-
tered great numbers of them at Gibeon and chased
the others all the way to Beth-horon and Azekah
and Makkedah, killing them along the way. And as
the enemy was racing down the hill to Beth-horon,
the Lord destroyed them with a great hailstorm
that continued all the way to Azekah; in fact, more
men died from the hail than by the swords of
the Israelis.

PRAYERS FOR GOD'S INTERVENTION

As the men of Israel were pursuing and harassing the foe, Joshua prayed aloud, "Let the sun stand still over Gibeon, and let the moon stand in its place over the valley of Aijalon!"

And the sun and the moon didn't move until the Israeli army had finished the destruction of its enemies!... So the sun stopped in the heavens and stayed there for almost twenty-four hours! There had never been such a day before, and there has never been another since, when the Lord stopped the sun and moon—all because of the prayer of one man. But the Lord was fighting for Israel.[6]

PRAYERS FOR
GOD'S HEALING

━━━━━━━━━━ ∽∾ ━━━━━━━━━━

Hezekiah became ill and was at the point of
death ... and prayed to the LORD,
"Remember, O LORD, how I have walked before you
faithfully and with wholehearted devotion and have
done what is good in your eyes."
The LORD replied, "I have heard your prayer and
seen your tears; I will heal you."

2 KINGS 20:1–3, 5

━━━━━━━━━━ ∽∾ ━━━━━━━━━━

No one ever looks in vain to the Great Physician.

F. F. BOSWORTH

I am the LORD, who heals you.

EXODUS 15:26

PRAYERS FOR GOD'S HEALING

THE GREAT PHYSICIAN

In August 2004, after bike riding with my family, I developed chest pain that wouldn't go away. So I drove myself to one of those Urgent Care clinics and had an EKG performed. With an abnormal result, they drove me to the ER in an ambulance. A doctor worked on me all night long, noticing anomalies everywhere that he called "bruits." I stayed nearly a week in the hospital undergoing a host of other tests. Finally, my cardiologist gave me a diagnosis—Takayasus Arteritus.

Takayasus Arteritus is an inflammation, scarring, and plaque buildup of the great vessels: the aorta, carotid, subclavian, and coronary arteries. Usually this autoimmune disease strikes Asian women, so how I, a white male, contracted it, is an interesting but unanswerable question. Four coronary stints and two years later, a piece of plaque lodged in an artery severing my left optic nerve. This eye stroke greatly concerned everyone, includ-

PRAYERS FOR
GOD'S HEALING

ing me. Radical surgery was demanded. So was radical prayer.

I didn't know how to pray for this event. I just knew I needed others to pray with me. So I sent out a mass email to all my friends asking for their prayers. My mother sent out an email to all her friends. And my grandfather sent one out to all his friends.

Buoyed by these prayers, I felt like Moses who had his hands raised over the fighting Israelites. As long as his hands were raised, the Israelites were victorious. When his hands were tired, others came along and propped his arms up. I felt that the prayers of others were propping me up too. People couldn't believe how peaceful I seemed despite the seriousness of my situation.

God also challenged me to pray his Word during my own personal prayer time. I took the Bible, opened it to Matthew, and found the parts where Jesus healed someone. When it came time for the "character" to speak with Jesus, I would

PRAYERS FOR GOD'S HEALING

stand up and recite these lines, envisioning Jesus before me as I spoke. Then I would read Jesus' words back to me, and I read the whole story this way until it was completed. If leprosy, blindness, or some other disease were mentioned, I'd substitute "Takayasus Arteritus" instead. I went through the whole Gospels praying this way, going over every story of healing as if I were the one approaching Jesus for the healing.

A few weeks later, an aorta specialist at the University of Michigan hospital told me the surgery would involve a partial aorta replacement, along with a total right carotid and subclavian replacement with artificial vessels. Chance of stroke or death was elevated. My faith in Christ and his love began to waver. I needed something more.

In the days before the surgery, I was working part-time at a Christian bookstore. Like any business, we got our fair share of junk mail. One mailing encouraged us to purchase Christian art. One postcard grabbed my attention and made me cry

PRAYERS FOR GOD'S HEALING

when I first saw it. Entitled "The Great Physician," the miniature painting depicted Jesus standing in an operating room, guiding the hand of the doctors. I carried that postcard around with me everywhere and looked at it often.

The day before I left for Ann Arbor for the surgery, my friends and I met for prayer. We all began with songs of praise and thanks to God. We decided that God was good and deserved praise, whatever would happen. What was my other option? Anger? Doubt? I knew these attitudes weren't healthy, and they wouldn't help me in any way.

After prayer, we went out for dinner where they told me Frankenstein jokes. This laughter also helped ease my tension. One friend, Sean, encouraged me the most, because he had lived through a drastic surgery removing a grapefruit-sized tumor on his brain. Long after everyone else left, Sean stayed to encourage me.

The morning of the surgery, my family and pastor met for prayer. Surprisingly, I wasn't even

Prayers for God's Healing

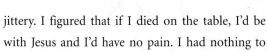

jittery. I figured that if I died on the table, I'd be with Jesus and I'd have no pain. I had nothing to lose. Fortunately, the surgery was a success.

Later, after the surgery, I showed my doctor the postcard of Jesus in the operating room. He said, "That's just the way it was." During that process, God gave me a new spiritual heart and new physical arteries. My blood flows much better now. And so does my gratitude and his love through me.[7]

PRAYERS FOR GOD'S HEALING

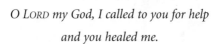

O LORD my God, I called to you for help
and you healed me.

PSALM 30:2

Our prayers lay the track down which God's power
can come. Like a mighty locomotive, his power is
irresistible, but it cannot reach us without rails.

WATCHMAN NEE

PRAYERS FOR GOD'S HEALING

PERFECT HEALING

Deep pain coursed through my abdomen. Gradually it lessened, only to be followed by continuing after-shocks. I begged God for relief. He sent intermittent reprieves, but the pain never totally disappeared. In fact, my agony seemed to escalate with each passing month.

Whenever the suffering threatened to incapacitate me, I asked my young daughters to pray for me. Their sweet entreaties for my health lifted my spirits even if the pain remained. Somehow I managed to get through each day, accomplishing at least the basics like cooking and laundry. I often sat with a heating pad and a pillow clutched over my stomach while my girls played at my feet.

I wondered if my husband, Ted, ever prayed for me. He claimed to want nothing to do with God, but I knew he cared for me. I shared my health struggles with the ladies' Bible study. They often interceded on my behalf. I requested prayer at church regarding my condition. My five-year-old

PRAYERS FOR GOD'S HEALING

daughter asked for prayer for me at her Christian school. My parents also upheld me in prayer.

With so many bringing my need for healing to the Lord, I wondered why he did not answer our pleas. Did I lack the necessary faith? I had been to several doctors and had tried medication, which no longer seemed very effective.

Feeling hopeless, I returned to my family physician. He said, "Since nothing we tried has worked, the only solution is a hysterectomy."

My mouth dropped open. *A hysterectomy? I* thought. *I'm only twenty-five years old!*

There appeared to be no alternative, so I went to see the surgeon. I liked Dr. Johnson right away. He seemed thorough, competent, and optimistic. After the exam, I got dressed and met him in his office. As soon as I was seated in the padded leather chair, he began: "I agree that a hysterectomy is needed. With cysts in both ovaries and chronic contractions of your uterus, you are not going to get better."

PRAYERS FOR GOD'S HEALING

We scheduled the surgery for June 23, the beginning of Ted's upcoming two-week vacation. That date also happened to be our seventh anniversary. *Oh well, I didn't feel much like celebrating anyway*, I thought.

As much I as I longed for relief, I felt nervous about undergoing such an operation. *Why couldn't God just heal me? It would bring him glory, and I would be glad to share such wonderful news.*

A friend invited me to a healing service at her church. I thought, *Why not? Maybe the Lord will still choose to heal me so I won't need surgery.*

While praying at the altar, I sensed God speaking to me. "I *can* heal you," he said. "But if you will go through with this surgery, I will use it to reach Ted."

I longed for Ted's salvation more than for my own health. I decided I had to undergo the surgery even if I could be healed without it. If that's what it took for Ted to come to the Lord, it would be worth it.

PRAYERS FOR
GOD'S HEALING

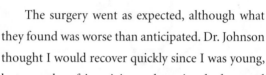

The surgery went as expected, although what they found was worse than anticipated. Dr. Johnson thought I would recover quickly since I was young, but months of inactivity and tension had sapped my strength. Then I developed another infection. My expected few days' stay dragged on and on.

My surgeon left for his vacation, turning over my care to his partner, Dr. Alley, whom I had never met. Tests showed my blood count had gone too low, so Dr. Alley ordered a blood transfusion. I thought such measures were only taken for seriously ill patients. Did this mean I might be dying?

I tried to call Ted, but no one answered at home. I phoned his grandparents, but they didn't know where he was. My parents and my pastor were out of town. I was on the verge of tears when the hospital chaplain came to pray with me.

Finally Ted arrived. He sat beside the bed and held my hand while cold, red blood entered my body through the IV. He tried to reassure me, but I could tell he was worried too.

PRAYERS FOR GOD'S HEALING

Ten days after surgery, I finally got to go home. The doctor ordered me to take walks to build up my strength. Ted walked with me since I was so weak.

On one of our daily walks through the neighborhood, Ted startled me by saying, "I think I'll start going to church with you." Ted shared how he had turned his life over to the Lord when he thought I might die.

Although God had promised he would accomplish this through my surgery, I could hardly believe it. How my heart rejoiced! I gripped Ted's hand tighter as we walked home together and thanked God for his amazing answer to prayer.[8]

PRAYERS FOR GOD'S HEALING

Prayer is the burden of a sigh,
The falling of a tear;
The upward glancing of an eye,
When none but God is near.

JAMES MONTGOMERY

I call on you, O God, for you will answer me;
give ear to me and hear my prayer.

PSALM 17:6

PRAYERS FOR GOD'S HEALING

HOLD ON!

"Freedom! I'm finally free. I can chart my own course, make my own decisions, and live my life the way I want. I'm finally twenty-one. Life is good."

The year was 1989, and I thought that I had won the lottery. I was free from the parental chains of bondage. I decided that I would indulge in the forbidden fruits my parents had warned me about—club parties and premarital sex. I dived into the wild life headfirst, convincing myself that at the end of the road I would find love, marriage, and happiness.

For five years I lived this way. I partied Thursday night through Sunday and occasionally I even went out on Tuesdays. I hung out with a new crowd and they were not Christians. They had no qualms about sleeping with strangers. My Christian roots would not allow me to fully embrace this ethic, but I decided that if I were in love, then sleeping with someone was acceptable.

The more I partied, the more depressed I got. I

PRAYERS FOR GOD'S HEALING

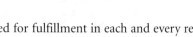

searched for fulfillment in each and every relationship, only to find that these men didn't really love me. They didn't care to know the real me.

I reached the end of my rope when I realized that I was sharing a married man. I continually sat by the phone hoping to hear from him, only to be disappointed when he didn't call. I settled for stolen moments that were both exhilarating and shameful. I knew he was not going to leave his wife and kids, but I secretly hoped he would.

One day I finally got it. I realized that life only has meaning if God is in it. I knelt on my bathroom floor and prayed, "Lord, if you are real, help me … please." I wanted happiness, love, peace, and a double dose of joy. The world and indulgent living had not lived up to its reputation. I was left wanting.

That day I poured out my heart to God. As tears cascaded down my cheeks, I prayed, "Lord, I've defiled my body. I've broken your commands. I've neglected myself. I've searched for love in the arms of men. I no longer want to live like that. I

PRAYERS FOR GOD'S HEALING

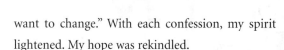

want to change." With each confession, my spirit lightened. My hope was rekindled.

It still amazes me that in just five short years, I had gone from being a twenty-one-year-old virgin to a woman living a loose lifestyle. Thankfully God still works on hard cases; he just requires a willing heart. Over the next few years, the Lord asked me to make some hard choices and implement new behaviors. "Dump Mr. Married Man. No stolen moments. No phone calls. Leave the party crew behind. Establish healthy friendships with women who have a godly point of view. Date only men who are willing to invest themselves and the time to get to know you, men who know Me. Learn to value yourself the way I value you."

At first it was awkward. I took one step forward and two steps back. But I refused to give up. I believed that God could do the impossible. As each year passed, I gained new hope. My faith grew. I no longer settled for pseudo-love. I held out for the real thing.

PRAYERS FOR GOD'S HEALING

In the late 1990s, God answered my prayer for a genuine loving relationship. He blessed me with Dwain, my best friend and now my husband. God has used Dwain to help me learn how to love, respect, and honor myself. God has opened my eyes through our marriage to the fact that love, sex, and marriage are inclusive. True joy comes when all components are there.

Every day I thank God for the blessing of love and emotional healing. What made the difference then, what makes the difference now, and what will make the difference in the future is God. My plan is simple. I will hold on to him for dear life.[9]

I hold on to you for dear life,
and you hold me steady as a post.

PSALM 63:8 MSG

PRAYERS FOR GOD'S HEALING

HOPE DEFERRED

I prayed, but God didn't answer. I didn't understand why.

As a new believer, I read my Bible. "Call on me and I will answer." I'd heard sermons that spoke of God's promises. "Ask and you will receive." I attended Bible study groups and church services where friends prayed for me. I took God at his Word. "If two or more agree on anything, it will be done." But it wasn't.

Instead, my condition grew worse. The chronic pain that began more than a decade earlier increased. One doctor's prognosis left little room for hope. "If you don't have the operation (to fuse your vertebrae), by the time you're thirty you'll be in a wheelchair." Still, I clung to God's promises.

Every time a visiting evangelist offered to pray for the sick, I dutifully went forward to stand in line. In large healing crusades, there were too many for individual prayer. So I stayed in my seat and

PRAYERS FOR GOD'S HEALING

did whatever the preacher instructed us to do. "Put your hand on the afflicted part of your body." But no matter what I did, nothing changed.

It was as if God were deaf. I often felt doubts. *Maybe I'm like the disciples; I don't believe enough.* I forgot that Jesus said I needed only the smallest amount of faith and that he has given each of us that measure of necessary faith. Other times I grew too tired to believe.

More years passed, and still I was not healed, though I watched God heal others. As a minister, I prayed for others, and God responded faithfully. At times, I prayed for relief from other afflictions, and God answered—once in a way that defied medical explanation. Yet the pain in my spine became almost intolerable.

Slowly, I grew indifferent.

When opportunities arose for prayer, I would grudgingly limp to the front of the church, let someone smear oil on my forehead, then return to my seat more bitter than before.

PRAYERS FOR GOD'S HEALING

More than ten years had passed since I first believed. My legs were partially paralyzed, my faith almost dead. Then, I decided to go with some friends to a miracle crusade.

We drove more than four hours to the convention center in a major metropolitan city. I knew God could heal me anywhere, at any time. I knew my healing didn't depend on the faith or charisma of a special person. I wanted to believe, and I was desperate enough to ask one more time.

The message was familiar: Only believe. From the passage about the Roman centurion, I heard about that man's great faith, and in response, I strained my feeble faith to hear God's voice.

When the minister read what the soldier said, "Only speak the Word," it was as if my mind heard God say, "I've already spoken my Word."

Those words seized my imagination. I understood what God meant. He spoke his creative Word and the universe existed. He spoke his Word and redemption was conceived in a virgin's womb. *If he*

PRAYERS FOR
GOD'S HEALING

did that, he can do this.

I felt my back. Where I could once stick half of my thumb into the indentation where the fifth lumbar vertebrae had slid forward some 75 percent, I felt only a small bump. Still tender, the pain suggested I was not healed. I almost doubted, but God's love conquered my fear.

Because I hadn't known a day without suffering, and the injured area remained extremely tender to the slightest touch, I found it difficult to accept that God had answered my prayer. *What if I say I'm healed, but I'm not?* I asked God.

God healed me that night, but more importantly, he strengthened my faith. I no longer feel a need to know *why*; it's enough to know that God loves me and his ways are perfect.

I still don't have answers to my questions. And I'm sure I'm not the only one who has asked. If God is all-powerful, and God has the power to heal, why must we wait; why must we suffer? These questions may not be answered until we see Jesus and know

PRAYERS FOR GOD'S HEALING

all in our heavenly home. I no longer need to know if or why God didn't answer me when I first prayed. I believe God answered that day.

Like the children of Israel in Egyptian bondage for four hundred years, God said, "I have heard their cries." For me, it's enough to know that he hears. I understand now that hope deferred is not hope denied.[10]

PRAYERS FOR GOD'S HEALING

Is any one of you sick? He should call the elders of the church to pray over him and anoint him with oil in the name of the Lord. And the prayer offered in faith will make the sick person well; the Lord will raise him up.

JAMES 5:14–15

The chief purpose of prayer is that God may be glorified in the answer.

R. A. TORREY

PRAYERS FOR
GOD'S HEALING

A SON TO HOLD

One day when Elisha came, he went up to his room and lay down there. He said to his servant Gehazi, "Call the Shunammite." So he called her, and she stood before him.

"What can be done for her?" Elisha asked.

Gehazi said, "Well, she has no son and her husband is old."

Then Elisha said, "Call her." So he called her, and she stood in the doorway. "About this time next year," Elisha said, "you will hold a son in your arms."

"No, my lord," she objected. "Don't mislead your servant, O man of God!"

But the woman became pregnant, and the next year about that same time she gave birth to a son, just as Elisha had told her.

The child grew, and one day he went out to his father, who was with the reapers. "My head! My head!" he said to his father.

PRAYERS FOR GOD'S HEALING

His father told a servant, "Carry him to his mother." After the servant had lifted him up and carried him to his mother, the boy sat on her lap until noon, and then he died. She went up and laid him on the bed of the man of God, then shut the door and went out.

So she set out and came to the man of God at Mount Carmel.

When he saw her in the distance, the man of God said to his servant Gehazi, "Look! There's the Shunammite! Run to meet her and ask her, 'Are you all right? Is your husband all right? Is your child all right?'"

"Everything is all right," she said.

When she reached the man of God at the mountain, she took hold of his feet…. "Did I ask you for a son, my lord?" she said. "Didn't I tell you, 'Don't raise my hopes'?"

Elisha said to Gehazi, "Tuck your cloak into your belt, take my staff in your hand and run. If you meet anyone, do not greet him, and if anyone greets

PRAYERS FOR
GOD'S HEALING

you, do not answer. Lay my staff on the boy's face."

Gehazi went on ahead and laid the staff on the boy's face, but there was no sound or response. So Gehazi went back to meet Elisha and told him, "The boy has not awakened."

When Elisha reached the house, there was the boy lying dead on his couch. He went in, shut the door on the two of them and prayed to the LORD. Then he got on the bed and lay upon the boy, mouth to mouth, eyes to eyes, hands to hands. As he stretched himself out upon him, the boy's body grew warm. Elisha turned away and walked back and forth in the room and then got on the bed and stretched out upon him once more. The boy sneezed seven times and opened his eyes.

Elisha summoned Gehazi and said, "Call the Shunammite." And he did. When she came, he said, "Take your son." She came in, fell at his feet and bowed to the ground.[11]

PRAYERS FOR GOD'S GUIDANCE

─────── ∽∂∽ ───────

Since you [O LORD] are my rock and my fortress,
for the sake of your name lead and guide me.

PSALM 31:3

─────── ∽∂∽ ───────

Prayer is the link between finite man and the infinite purposes of God.... To pray in the truest sense means to put our lives into total conformity with what God desires.

PAT ROBERTSON

How gracious [the LORD] will be when you cry for help! As soon as he hears, he will answer you.... Whether you turn to the right or to the left, your ears will hear a voice behind you, saying, "This is the way; walk in it."

ISAIAH 30:19, 21

PRAYERS FOR GOD'S GUIDANCE

A PRAYER FOR GOD'S BEST

All my life I had been told, and as a result fully believed, I was born with a God-given purpose. But at twenty-three years of age and nearly five years into my marriage, I found my life going nowhere. I kept thinking, *There has to be more!* Somehow—somewhere I must have stepped off God's road map for my life. A fire burned within me to get back on track.

After sharing my feelings with my husband, Blaine, I learned that he was feeling the same way. We concluded we were not where we should be in the life journey God had sketched out for us. We had a knowing in our hearts that if we stayed where we were we would miss God's best for our lives.

One evening, we were again discussing our situation when an image of Grandma's prayer times came back to me.

As a young girl while visiting my grandma, I had witnessed the power of prayer. I recalled my grandmother standing in the living room of

PRAYERS FOR GOD'S GUIDANCE

her double-wide mobile home praying for the Oklahoma tornadoes to pass over, while I reluctantly climbed down into the basement with Grandpa and my cousins. The tornadoes always passed over and never touched my grandparents' land. I remember waking up in the morning to my grandma's voice calling out to God, kneeling at the edge of her neatly made bed. Her faith to see God move in the lives of her family members was a testimony to me.

I looked at Blaine holding our two-year-old son on his lap. "We need to pray about this," I told him, "right now!" We had come into agreement for our situation—as individuals and as a couple—and we sealed it in prayer. We made a commitment to listen and watch for God's perfect will, and we went to bed expecting to hear from him.

The next morning (Monday) we headed to work. We each had a forty-minute commute, during which I always listened to the local Christian radio station. That morning, I heard an announce-

Prayers for God's Guidance

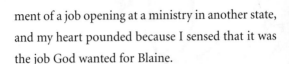

ment of a job opening at a ministry in another state, and my heart pounded because I sensed that it was the job God wanted for Blaine.

When I got to work, I called the radio station and got the information about the job they had advertised. The next day (Tuesday) Blaine mailed his résumé to that organization—a worldwide ministry. On Friday—five days after we had prayed—they called him. He went for an interview the following Friday and was offered the job. Five weeks from the night we prayed, we packed our two-year-old son and few belongings in a U-Haul and set out on the most amazing adventure of our lives.

That one prayer turned our lives right-side up—placing us directly on God's path for our lives—and we're still on it.

He never lets us miss a beat as long as we are willing to walk with him toward our destiny. And we know that even when we make a wrong turn, which we all do from time to time, if we will run

PRAYERS FOR GOD'S GUIDANCE

to him and ask, he'll set our feet back on the right course and turn us in the right direction.[12]

Prayer is none other but the revelation of the will or mind of God.

JOHN SALTMARSH

[Jesus] knelt down and prayed, "Father, if you are willing, take this cup from me; yet not my will, but yours be done."

LUKE 22:41–42

PRAYERS FOR GOD'S GUIDANCE

THANK YOU, LORD

In 1996, God called me to be a counselor at a Christian camp for abused and abandoned children, but I felt completely unequipped for that position. Those precious kids needed someone with more skills than I could bring to the job.

At a ladies' prayer meeting one night, we broke off into groups. I heard the other women in my group praying, but I was distracted, still thinking about the camp. My heart would not settle down, so I asked him, *How can you possibly ask me to do this? I'm not trained to be a counselor!* And then I distinctly heard the words: *My child, I want you to do this for me.*

How could I ignore that? I bowed to God's greatness and silently whispered my thanks to him for being so patient with me. And then I prayed one last thing: *God, if you really want me to do this, please enable me for the task.*

Four short months later, I was at camp. One of the little girls was a particularly tough case. Eight-

PRAYERS FOR GOD'S GUIDANCE

year-old Debbie had been shuffled from one foster home to another. She was certain of only one thing: that she could expect abuse or negative treatment on a regular basis. Like so many of these children, she learned to bury her true emotions and instead developed a defensive posture.

Debbie's stubbornness was not easy for any of us to deal with. Whenever we were to start anything new—crafts, chapel, or even games—Debbie's standard response was "No!" She would hunker down and shout this over and over again. I found myself praying almost constantly that week.

Our goal was to give these children a week of carefree fun, but Debbie's tantrums kept testing both my patience and that of the camp directors. After several days of this negative behavior, we had a discussion about sending Debbie home early. This upset me greatly. How could we take away this one week of enjoyment from someone who needed it so desperately? I asked the directors to give her another chance and they agreed.

PRAYERS FOR GOD'S GUIDANCE

That night, I found myself unable to sleep because of Debbie's noisy night terrors. She tossed and turned as she relived some terrifying experiences, and mumbled "Don't!" and "Stop!" continuously. After over an hour of listening to this, I began to pray. I asked him to help me understand Debbie and give me the key to her troubled heart.

The Lord showed me that Debbie's life was full of commands; no one ever asked her if she *wanted* to do anything. God then gave me one word—*choices*—and showed me that if Debbie were given some limited choices, she might respond differently.

The next day, Debbie started her usual tantrum when informed it was time for chapel. Before she could get carried away, I offered her a choice: Go with me to chapel or to the nurse's office. Of course, she chose to stay with the nurse, but not more than fifteen minutes later, I felt a tap on my shoulder, and there stood Debbie. "I want to be here with you," she whispered.

PRAYERS FOR GOD'S GUIDANCE

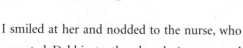

I smiled at her and nodded to the nurse, who had escorted Debbie to the chapel. As we stood to sing, I felt Debbie's small hand slip into mine. *Thank you, Lord.*

I pray that I will always be willing to answer God's call to walk "by faith." To do otherwise is to miss a huge blessing!

By the way, Debbie is now sixteen years old and can't wait for her turn to be a counselor at camp.[13]

> *Lord, lead me as you promised me*
> *you would....*
> *Tell me clearly what to do.*
>
> PSALM 5:8 TLB

PRAYERS FOR GOD'S GUIDANCE

THE RIGHT PLACE FOR MOTHER

The last week of March seemed like it would never end. I was frustrated and frightened. Exhausted, I lay on my bed blinking away tears. My body ached, yet I had little time to rest. Much like a parent with a newborn, I was taking a break while the "child" slept.

"Lord, what do I do now?" The tears trickled down my temples and into my hair. "I need direction. I don't want to make a mistake. Please tell me what to do."

As my mother's primary caretaker, I had to make the crucial decision: Was putting her in a nursing home the best option for all of us? She had begged me so often in years past to let her die at home, yet physically I couldn't care for her anymore. I knew I had to have more help to create a safer environment for both of us.

The following morning, I took the first step and paid a visit to a nearby nursing home. It was

PRAYERS FOR GOD'S GUIDANCE

within a half mile of my house, and I was surprised to see how nice and clean it was. Cheerful nurses greeted patients parked in wheelchairs about the foyer. *Maybe this wouldn't be so bad*, I thought at first, but then I realized that although they could provide for her *needs*, they wouldn't necessarily know her *wants*.

On the one hand, I'd spoiled my mom and enjoyed doing so. At home, she slept late, and I served her breakfast when she awoke. During the day, she was used to ice cream on demand, peanut butter and jelly sandwiches cut in triangles, and a chocolate-chip cookie with her medications. Could overwhelmed nurses provide her with the care I could?

On the other hand, Alzheimer's had eaten away so much of who she was, and her ability to function disintegrated daily. I had now become the parent of my parent, and the job was taking its toll.

Back home, in the silence of my bedroom, I cried out, "Lord, you've told us to honor our moth-

PRAYERS FOR GOD'S GUIDANCE

ers and fathers. I want to be obedient. I don't know what to do." I clutched my Bible to my chest, wanting its words to penetrate my weary soul.

"Father," I prayed, "I know my mother's days are in your hands, so please direct me and guide me to care for her to the best of my ability."

Within my heart, the words, *Wait until the first of the month*, resonated. At first I assumed it was just my own procrastination, hoping to delay a decision.

I prayed again, "Father, you tell us that you will not give us more than we can bear. Give me direction, Lord. I choose to follow you."

Again, *Wait until the first of the month*, entered my thoughts. "Okay, Jesus, that's one week away. I'm going to trust that these thoughts are from you."

My faith strengthened, I struggled to my feet and returned to my mom's bedside for another sleepless night. And I waited.

Saturday, April 1 dawned brightly. Reluctantly, I picked up the phone directory and dialed the

PRAYERS FOR GOD'S GUIDANCE

new nursing home I'd chosen. Within minutes, my mother's name was on the waiting list. My heart wrenched as I felt I had betrayed her.

Later that morning, my sister arrived so I could get some rest. After a short nap, she startled me awake and called me to our mother's room. "I think she's gotten worse," she said. "Can you call the nurse?"

Mother had hospice care throughout the last few months, so I dialed their number and asked them to send a nurse. She arrived, assessed the situation, and insisted that we move our mother to their in-patient hospital facility for better care. It was her opinion that our mom had suffered a stroke.

Minutes later, an ambulance arrived and whisked her away to a private room at the nursing home. When I saw it, I was amazed. Her room was on a lovely secluded floor. No hospital setting. No nursing home smells. Beautiful furnishings and décor met our eyes.

PRAYERS FOR GOD'S GUIDANCE

Despite the one-on-one care, my mother never regained consciousness and died a few days later. But I knew God had answered my prayer for guidance. He had said, "Wait one more week," knowing that he would soon be taking my mother to heaven. She would never need that nursing home, because God had better plans for her. She is now in his presence, well indeed.[14]

PRAYERS FOR GOD'S GUIDANCE

I am always with you;

you hold me by my right hand.

You guide me with your counsel.

PSALM 73:23–24

Prayer means that I am to be raised up into feeling,
into union and design with him; that I am to enter
into his counsel and carry out his purpose fully.

DWIGHT LYMAN MOODY

PRAYERS FOR GOD'S GUIDANCE

IN TRANSITION

When I was newly married, I worked as a reception-ist for a local firm. My husband and I soon decided that I needed a job with better pay and benefits, so the search began for a new job. When the right job came along, I was excited. But my enthusiasm didn't last long. I was barely settling in when my boss asked me to work different hours—it was not a large change in time, but it was enough to cut into my evenings. Soon we were back where we had started—praying for another job.

This time we prayed for direction. We now realized that without the Lord's guidance, we could end up going from job to job never finding the right place. I wanted to be in the center of God's will.

For the next month, I prayed for favor with my boss and colleagues. I also prayed that God would show me how to be a better employee and do my job more efficiently.

Several weeks after we began praying about this matter, I felt the Lord saying that my job would be

PRAYERS FOR GOD'S GUIDANCE

coming to an end—and he wanted me to start my own housecleaning business. I couldn't have been more shocked! I had never dreamed of working for myself, but I began to ponder the possibility. I told my husband, and we both started praying for confirmation on the matter.

Within two weeks, I was called into the office at work and told that the company was downsizing. My position had been eliminated, but another position with less pay and benefits was offered.

When I told my husband the news, we agreed that it was the confirmation we had asked for.

I received my first two clients from the office where I had worked. Then I decided to run an ad in the local newspaper. I used a few catchy lines, and the business began coming in.

Since that time, I have been divinely planted in many homes where the people were not Christians. Many of these people were experiencing depression, alcoholism, suicidal thoughts, health crises, and marital problems. The list goes on and on. I have

PRAYERS FOR GOD'S GUIDANCE

had the privilege of leading the elderly to Christ, praying for the sick and disheartened, counseling women on numerous issues, and showing love to children who had been neglected. I quickly learned to pray for each family as I cleaned their houses.

In one situation, I began a job for a woman whose husband had left her and her two children for another woman some thirty years prior. Since that time, she had fallen deeper and deeper into depression and alcoholism.

As I encouraged her that God loved her and cherished her, in fact, she began to lessen her hold on alcohol. As I continued to talk to her about God, telling her that she was of great value to him, she began to open up. We had many talks after my work was done, and one wonderful day I was able to pray the prayer of salvation with her. Within six months, she passed away, and I knew that I had been part of her miracle. God had used me to extend his love to her. It was a great honor.[15]

PRAYERS FOR GOD'S GUIDANCE

Just tell me what to do and I will do it, Lord.

As long as I live I'll wholeheartedly obey.

PSALM 119:33–34 TLB

There is nothing that makes us love a man so much

as praying for him.

WILLIAM LAW

PRAYERS FOR GOD'S GUIDANCE

CONSIDER THIS PERSON

Mona, a woman in my church, had pushed us all to the brink. She had taken it upon herself to act as the "boss" of every group discussion in which she participated. If she thought that one person had been speaking too long, she would point it out, saying that someone else should be given a chance. She would complain when she thought people were straying from the subject. She frequently embarrassed shy people by blurting out, "I want to hear what *he* has to say!" leaving the taciturn person speechless and humiliated. Worst of all, she would tell those who were thinking of going into some new ministry that they really didn't have what it would take to succeed.

I felt justified in my resolution that difficult as it would be, I was going to be the one to set Mona straight. Fortunately I remembered to pray about this before going ahead with it.

Dear God, I prayed, *Mona is driving me and the others crazy. Is it your will that I confront her, and if*

PRAYERS FOR GOD'S GUIDANCE

so, what should I say?

God's answer was frustratingly brief and simple: *Consider this person.*

Against my own instincts and wishes, I put off confronting Mona until I could understand her a little better. What I discovered astounded me. Mona had grown up with an older sister who had bullied her both physically and verbally. Her sister had criticized her every move. Most illuminating was that this sister had talked incessantly, never allowing others to get a word in edgewise as she expounded her misinformed views. I understood why Mona was so critical of others and why she always tried to control conversations.

I realized that confrontation was not what was needed. As I relaxed and became more tolerant of Mona's behavior, I began to notice things about her I hadn't seen before. She eventually abandoned discouraging people in their ministries and began encouraging people even when early results were not promising. Her feedback on sermons revealed

PRAYERS FOR GOD'S GUIDANCE

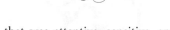

a mind that was attentive, sensitive, and insightful. My love for her grew as Christ showed me her beauty.

I thank God that he sets us straight, especially when we're most certain we're in the right. What unnecessary hurt I would have caused had I followed my own understanding! *Consider this person* is something I remind myself of now every time someone annoys me. I ask God to guide me, enlighten me, and teach me to see as he sees and love as he loves.[16]

PRAYERS FOR GOD'S GUIDANCE

I have asked the Lord for one thing;
one thing only do I want: to live in
the Lord's house all my life,
to marvel there at his goodness, and to
ask for his guidance.

PSALM 27:4 GNT

Be thou a bright flame before me,
Be thou a guiding star above me,
Be thou a smooth path below me,
And be a kindly Shepherd behind me,
Today, tonight and forever.

ALEXANDER CARMICHAEL

PRAYERS FOR GOD'S GUIDANCE

INSTRUCTIONS FOR A SPECIAL SON

One day the Angel of the Lord appeared to the wife of Manoah, of the tribe of Dan, who lived in the city of Zorah. She had no children, but the Angel said to her, "Even though you have been barren so long, you will soon conceive and have a son! Don't drink any wine or beer and don't eat any food that isn't kosher. Your son's hair must never be cut, for he shall be a Nazirite, a special servant of God from the time of his birth; and he will begin to rescue Israel from the Philistines."

The woman ran and told her husband, "A man from God appeared to me and I think he must be the Angel of the Lord, for he was almost too glorious to look at. I didn't ask where he was from, and he didn't tell me his name, but he told me, 'You are going to have a baby boy!' …

Then Manoah prayed, "O Lord, please let the man from God come back to us again and give us more instructions about the child you are going

PRAYERS FOR GOD'S GUIDANCE

to give us." The Lord answered his prayer, and the Angel of God appeared once again to his wife as she was sitting in the field. But again she was alone — Manoah was not with her — so she quickly ran and found her husband and told him, "The same man is here again!"

Manoah ran back with his wife and asked,… "Can you give us any special instructions about how we should raise the baby after he is born?"

And the Angel replied, "Be sure that your wife follows the instructions I gave her. She must not eat grapes or raisins, or drink any wine or beer, or eat anything that isn't kosher."

Then Manoah said to the Angel, "Please stay here until we can get you something to eat."

"I'll stay," the Angel replied, "but I'll not eat anything. However, if you wish to bring something, bring an offering to sacrifice to the Lord."…

Then Manoah asked him for his name. "When all this comes true and the baby is born," he said to the Angel, "we will certainly want to tell everyone

PRAYERS FOR GOD'S GUIDANCE

that you predicted it!"

"Don't even ask my name," the Angel replied, "for it is a secret."

Then Manoah took a young goat and a grain offering and offered it as a sacrifice to the Lord; and the Angel did a strange and wonderful thing, for as the flames from the altar were leaping up toward the sky, and as Manoah and his wife watched, the Angel ascended in the fire! Manoah and his wife fell face downward to the ground, and that was the last they ever saw of him. It was then that Manoah finally realized that it had been the Angel of the Lord.[17]

Prayers for God's Protection

God's angel sets up a circle of protection around us while we pray.

Psalm 34:7 MSG

*[Prayer] is the key that shuts us up under his
protection and safeguard.*

JACQUES ELLUL

*I come to you, Lord, for protection; ... save me,
I pray!... Hear me! Save me now!*

PSALM 31:1–2 GNT

PRAYERS FOR GOD'S PROTECTION

235 PRAYERS ANSWERED

February 2, 1979, started out like any ordinary day. I began the day by loading up on a commercial airline chartered for my unit, the 2/69th Armor Battalion as part of the 197th Infantry Brigade. Our unit was venturing forth on a mission to Fort Drum, New York, for Winter Warfare Training.

The day seemed calm as we boarded our flight. Temperatures were in the sixties, and even though it was cloudy on the ground, it was sunny at forty thousand feet. I loved flying, and as the plane soared into the air, thoughts of prayer were far from my mind. That attitude would soon change.

During the flight, the captain told us there was a major winter storm hitting the Fort Drum area. These circumstances had forced him to divert the flight to LaGuardia Airport. But after circling the airport for some time, it was determined that the conditions were too bad for us to land at either LaGuardia or Kennedy airports. After circling the state of New York for another hour, Niagara Falls

PRAYERS FOR GOD'S PROTECTION

Airport finally told us that they would deice their airfield so we could land there.

On the first attempt to land, our plane passed into the dark clouds, and then the snow. I could just make out the faint runway lights to my left and felt one side of the wheels touch down when a huge gust of wind struck the fuselage, and I felt the aircraft turn.

I stayed right at my window and watched as the runway lights were no longer passing under the wing of the plane. I yelled out, "We're skidding sideways!"

Suddendly, the need for earnest prayer became obvious! We were skidding down an airstrip, and never in my few short years had I ever heard of a plane surviving such a severe turn of events.

Two hundred and thirty-five passengers began to pray. The most prevalent prayer was, "Please, God, I don't want to die! Please save us!" This seemed to be the most effective and direct prayer addressing a grave situation, and this one called

PRAYERS FOR GOD'S PROTECTION

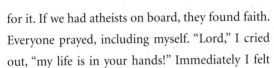

for it. If we had atheists on board, they found faith. Everyone prayed, including myself. "Lord," I cried out, "my life is in your hands!" Immediately I felt peace—I knew I was ready to meet my maker.

Suddenly the engines on one side of the plane reversed turbines, and the plane lurched back in alignment with the airstrip. The pilot reversed both engines at that point and the brakes managed to stop the plane just before we plowed into the pile of snow at the end of the runway.

The pilot came over the air and said, almost comically, "Thank you for flying with our airline. I hope you enjoyed your flight."

A round of applause rang forth as every passenger aboard praised the pilot for saving our lives. I did not clap. I felt their praise was not going to the One to whom everyone had been praying just moments ago. I had witnessed the power of prayer, and I gave credit to God for his miraculous intervention in our lives.

Soon, directions to exit the plane through the

PRAYERS FOR GOD'S PROTECTION

emergency doors were given, because the plane still presented imminent danger. When I reached the ground, I gazed back through the limited visibility expecting to see twisted landing gear and at least minor damage to the fuselage of the aircraft — but to my surprise, it was as if nothing had happened.

I will always remember the time I experienced the seriousness of a plane crash and knew my Savior was with me. I knew he would handle it, whether he calmed the storm around me or the storm within me.[18]

The Lord says, "Because he loves me, I will rescue him; I will make him great because he trusts in my name. When he calls on me, I will answer; I will be with him in trouble and rescue him and honor him."

PSALM 91:14–15 TLB

PRAYERS FOR GOD'S PROTECTION

GIVE US THIS DAY OUR DAILY BREAD

Twenty-five years ago, my husband, Mike, nearly died of meningitis. It took him months to recover his strength. After he finally felt like himself again, we discovered that he had developed epilepsy because the meningitis had damaged his brain. He consulted a neurologist, who prescribed anti-seizure medicines.

The drugs worked, up to a point. But once in a while, he would have a "breakthrough seizure," usually mild and not noticeable to other people. Occasionally he would have a bigger seizure that would last longer, which was not only noticeable to others but also potentially dangerous in certain circumstances. No adjustment of drugs seemed to prevent this from happening.

From the beginning, we prayed that the condition would be healed, but to no avail. We were appalled when well-meaning friends cited the biblical story of the epileptic boy in Matthew 17 and

PRAYERS FOR GOD'S PROTECTION

then proceeded to pray (unsuccessfully, and usually loudly) for Mike to be delivered from evil spirits. We eventually learned that it was best not to talk about the whole thing; it carried a disturbing stigma. It was, like Paul's "thorn in the flesh," a perpetually humbling ailment. Mike (and I) learned to accept it as such, although we always held out some hope for a complete healing.

The breakthrough seizures continued to be a problem. What if he had one while driving the car? We reasoned that he always had enough warning from the preliminary "aura" to ensure that he could pull off the road and wait it out safely. Even so, it was a worrisome situation. What if he someday found himself on a stretch of highway with no shoulder on which to pull off? Also, once or twice over the years, he had a breakthrough seizure at work or in public. It was more than humbling—it was humiliating.

Finally, in addition to the prescription drugs, a special kind of prayer became our "drug of choice."

PRAYERS FOR GOD'S PROTECTION

This prayer needed to be "taken" daily, just as the other medicines were. We felt it was in keeping with the line from the Lord's Prayer, "give us this day our daily bread."

Since our wedding night, Mike and I have always prayed together at bedtime. Mike prays for me and I for him, and we both pray for our four children (now young adults) and other concerns. Now I began to pray a very simple nightly request: "Lord, please prevent Mike from having any seizures tomorrow while driving, at work, or in public."

Because the seizures were only occasional, it took a while to see results. But Mike soon began to report that any breakthrough seizures he had were occurring safely at home, even during his sleep. This was good news! I kept up the daily prayers.

A few years went by. One spring day, we flew to another state for a conference. At our destination, we rented a car and began to drive into the city on an unfamiliar expressway. Suddenly, Mike stepped on the gas for no apparent reason. "You're going

PRAYERS FOR GOD'S PROTECTION

kind of fast," I said as I glanced over at him—only to find that he was in the throes of a grand mal seizure! "Jesus, Jesus, Jesus, help!"

It was obvious why he hadn't pulled over—the expressway was hemmed in by concrete walls. The road was relatively straight, and traffic was light, but Mike's hands were locked on the wheel and his right foot was flooring the gas pedal. We were gaining rapidly on an unsuspecting driver in another car.

I reached across the seat and wrested the wheel from Mike's tight hold. With all my strength, I managed to keep the car on the road, steering it around the other car, all the while talking to Mike in case he could begin to respond to my words: "Mike, you're having a seizure. Let me steer." Adding to the nightmarish situation, it began to rain, and I could no longer see what was ahead. But I could not let go of the wheel to turn on the windshield wipers. For what seemed like forever, we hurtled down the slick road at 100 miles per hour.

PRAYERS FOR GOD'S PROTECTION

Eventually, the seizure ended, and I talked Mike through to an exit. I was completely undone, exhausted, and scared speechless. Because of the effects of the seizure, Mike remembered almost nothing.

That night, I realized that this had been a wake-up call. The trip preparations had altered our prayer routine the night before. Apparently, my nightly prayers really had been effective. So I resumed praying with renewed conviction. To date, prayers have eliminated public seizures.

We're still holding out for a complete healing someday, although after 25 years it's difficult for us to believe that it could happen. Surely God is big enough. My faith isn't—except for this kind of daily praying. I feel that these prayers match my level of faith; night after night, I'm making a "faith-sized" request.

Meantime, we're always growing in maturity and responsiveness to God. Prayer is a two-way

PRAYERS FOR GOD'S PROTECTION

communication. Should he ever indicate that we should pray for something bigger and bolder, I want to be paying attention.[19]

Protect me as you would the pupil of your eye;
hide me in the shadow of your wings as you
hover over me.

PSALM 17:8 TLB

There is no greater place of safety than in the
shadow of the Almighty. A simple prayer secures the
Christian's place there.

MERIWETHER WILLIAMS

PRAYERS FOR GOD'S PROTECTION

DAVID'S PRAYER FOR SAFETY

One day as Saul was sitting at home, listening to David playing the harp, suddenly the tormenting spirit from the Lord attacked him. He had his spear in his hand and hurled it at David in an attempt to kill him. But David dodged out of the way and fled into the night, leaving the spear imbedded in the timber of the wall. Saul sent troops to watch David's house and kill him when he came out in the morning.

"If you don't get away tonight," Michal warned him, "you'll be dead by morning."

So she helped him get down to the ground through a window. Then she took an idol and put it in his bed, and covered it with blankets, with its head on a pillow of goat's hair.

Written by David at the time King Saul set guards at his home to capture and kill him.

O my God, save me from my enemies. Protect me from these who have come to destroy me. Preserve me from these criminals, these murderers.

PRAYERS FOR GOD'S PROTECTION

They lurk in ambush for my life. Strong men are out there waiting. And not, O Lord, because I've done them wrong. Yet they prepare to kill me. Lord, waken! See what is happening! Help me!

O God my Strength! I will sing your praises, for you are my place of safety. My God is changeless in his love for me, and he will come and help me. He will let me see my wish come true upon my enemies. Don't kill them—for my people soon forget such lessons—but stagger them with your power and bring them to their knees.

When the soldiers came to arrest David and take him to Saul, [Michal] told them he was sick and couldn't get out of bed. Saul said to bring him in his bed, then, so that he could kill him. But when they came to carry him out, they discovered that it was only an idol!

"Why have you deceived me and let my enemy escape?" Saul demanded of Michal.

"I had to," Michal replied. "He threatened to kill me if I didn't help him."

PRAYERS FOR GOD'S PROTECTION

In that way David got away and went to Ramah to see Samuel, and told him all that Saul had done to him. So Samuel took David with him to live at Naioth. When the report reached Saul that David was at Naioth in Ramah, he sent soldiers to capture him; but when they arrived and saw Samuel and the other prophets prophesying, the Spirit of God came upon them and they also began to prophesy. When Saul heard what had happened, he sent other soldiers, but they too prophesied! The same thing happened a third time! Then Saul himself went to Ramah and arrived at the great well in Secu.

"Where are Samuel and David?" he demanded.

Someone told him they were at Naioth. But on the way to Naioth the Spirit of God came upon Saul, and he too began to prophesy!

This song of David was written at a time when the Lord had delivered him from his many enemies, including Saul:

Lord, how I love you! For you have done such tremendous things for me.

PRAYERS FOR GOD'S PROTECTION

The Lord is my fort where I can enter and be safe; no one can follow me in and slay me. He is a rugged mountain where I hide; he is my Savior, a rock where none can reach me, and a tower of safety. He is my shield. He is like the strong horn of a mighty fighting bull. All I need to do is cry to him — oh, praise the Lord — and I am saved from all my enemies!

Death bound me with chains, and the floods of ungodliness mounted a massive attack against me. Trapped and helpless, I struggled against the ropes that drew me on to death.

In my distress I screamed to the Lord for his help. And he heard me from heaven; my cry reached his ears.

He reached down from heaven and took me and drew me out of my great trials. He rescued me from deep waters. He delivered me from my strong enemy, from those who hated me — I who was helpless in their hands.

PRAYERS FOR GOD'S PROTECTION

On the day when I was weakest, they attacked. But the Lord held me steady. He led me to a place of safety, for he delights in me.[20]

Let everyone who is godly pray to you
while you may be found;
surely when the mighty waters rise,
they will not reach him.
You are my hiding place;
you will protect me from trouble and
surround me with songs of deliverance.

PSALM 32:6–7

PRAYERS FOR GOD'S PROVISION

———— ∽∾ ————

Jesus prayed,
"Our Father in heaven,
hallowed be your name,
Give us today our daily bread."

MATTHEW 6:9, 11

———— ∽∾ ————

There is no need too great for God.
He has unlimited resources at his disposal,
and he delights in making them available to
his children. All we have to do is ask.

MERIWETHER WILLIAMS

You, Lord, are all I have, and you give me all I need;
my future is in your hands.

PSALM 16:5 GNT

PRAYERS FOR GOD'S PROVISION

BETTY JO PRAYERS

Betty Jo taught me more about praying for my children just by being herself than she ever knew. I watched her spend eighteen or twenty years teaching, modeling, and mentoring her children before I became a mother myself. I'm sure now that it took long hours, hard work, and sometimes thankless effort, but she never let it show. She went about mothering with laughter, common sense, and daily prayer to God about each of her children. I watched her four children grow up and eventually choose marriage partners with values and faith, and I knew that was what I wanted for my two children too.

One day at church I asked Betty Jo, "How did it happen that each of your four children chose such great people to marry?"

Without hesitating, she replied, "Why, when they were still babies, I started praying for the person they would choose as their husband or wife. They will spend many more years with the person

PRAYERS FOR GOD'S PROVISION

they select to marry than they would ever spend with me!"

This a new concept for me! Most of my prayers were along the lines of, "Lord, help me not to scream if I have to change one more diaper!" I had never thought much about praying for my children's futures, let alone their future mates.

Betty Jo and I never mentioned that conversation again. I didn't tell others about the message I had received from God through her. I certainly didn't tell my children; they were too small to understand. I simply started doing it—praying day by day for the marriage partners each of our two children would choose.

That was the beginning, but it didn't stop there. While reading 2 Timothy one day, I realized that the verses Paul had written to his "son" in the ministry could also become my prayers. There I found Paul suggesting certain godly traits; I began to list them in my journal. I found myself praying for these same characteristics to develop in my children

PRAYERS FOR GOD'S PROVISION

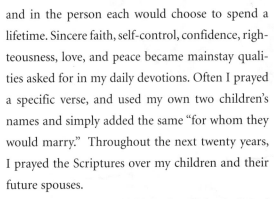

and in the person each would choose to spend a lifetime. Sincere faith, self-control, confidence, righteousness, love, and peace became mainstay qualities asked for in my daily devotions. Often I prayed a specific verse, and used my own two children's names and simply added the same "for whom they would marry." Throughout the next twenty years, I prayed the Scriptures over my children and their future spouses.

On each of their wedding days, I thanked God for his answers to my "Betty Jo prayers." Both of our children, as well as their marriage partners, are certainly individuals with talents and minds of their own, but they serve God faithfully. Now, after five years of marriage for our daughter and her husband, and after seven years for our son and his wife, I am so grateful for the answer to my prayers. I look at these beautiful young adults and marvel, "These are the persons for whom I prayed!"

Twenty-five years have come and gone since that short conversation with Betty Jo. She is no

PRAYERS FOR GOD'S PROVISION

longer alive on this earth. Her great-grandchildren are my grandchildren's ages, just toddlers. But what better time to start praying "Betty Jo prayers" for them?[21]

> *When in prayer you clasp your hands,*
> *God opens his.*
>
> GERMAN PROVERB

> *Don't worry about anything; instead,*
> *pray about everything; tell God your needs,*
> *and don't forget to thank him*
> *for his answers.*
>
> PHILIPPIANS 4:6 TLB

PRAYERS FOR GOD'S PROVISION

GUARDIAN ANGEL

It was one of life's magical moments granted by the mysterious grace of God. While raindrops gently falling from the midnight sky danced across the windowpane, soft light bathed a corner of the dim hospital room. Serenity saturated my heart as my husband and I exchanged silent glances. With quiet joy we celebrated the moment—and the miracle of our newborn daughter's birth.

Barely an hour old, she lay cradled in my arms. Gratitude to God filled my soul as I gazed in silent wonder into her precious face. I marveled as I realized the intensity of my affection for this precious child and considered the unsurpassable love the Heavenly Father has lavished upon his children!

"Time to get this little lady back to the nursery," said the rosy-cheeked nurse who appeared at my bedside. She carefully placed my baby into the crib and rolled the cart down the hall.

It was nearly midnight, and I smiled at my bleary-eyed husband nodding off in the wooden

PRAYERS FOR GOD'S PROVISION

rocker. "The third shift nurse will be in soon," I said softly. "Why don't you head home and get some sleep?"

Bryant gathered his gear. "I love you," he said with a tender kiss and a smile. "See you in the morning."

I soon drifted into a deep sleep, barely noticing my nurse's frequent exams. I'd had a routine delivery, but while I was sleeping, complications developed.

"Cindy," a gentle voice in the darkness called, coaxing me awake. "This is Betty, your nurse," she said. "Hon, your bleeding is heavier than normal. I called your doctor and he's ordered an injection." In my groggy state, her words slowly started to sink in.

Fatigue and medication clouded my thinking. Fear took control of my mind. Thoughts darted frantically from my newborn in the nursery, to my precious three-year-old sleeping peacefully at my parents' home. *Will I ever see them again?* I wondered, anxiety spinning out of control.

PRAYERS FOR GOD'S PROVISION

I grabbed the phone to call Bryant. As I heard the dial tone, my eye caught a glimpse of the clock. It was 3:05 a.m. Should I wake him only to worry him—at this hour!?

Scared and alone, my emotions surged, sweeping over me like a tidal wave. Tears tumbled down my cheeks. Soon, a woman appeared in the dim light, golden curls framing her delicate face. Smiling, she sat down in the chair by the bed and spoke in a soothing voice I recognized at once.

"As a Christian," Betty began, "I truly believe in the power of prayer." I forced a weak smile in agreement.

"May I pray with you?" she asked, patting my hand. I nodded.

Betty tenderly asked Jesus to fill my heart with his perfect peace and restore my body by his healing touch. "May Your angels surround her to comfort and protect," she prayed.

As she spoke, my fears subsided.

A sudden crescendo of clattering jostled me

PRAYERS FOR GOD'S PROVISION

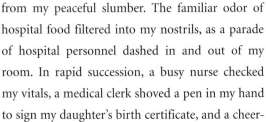

from my peaceful slumber. The familiar odor of hospital food filtered into my nostrils, as a parade of hospital personnel dashed in and out of my room. In rapid succession, a busy nurse checked my vitals, a medical clerk shoved a pen in my hand to sign my daughter's birth certificate, and a cheerful candy striper placed a breakfast tray under my nose. Staring at the bland meal, I wondered about my fearful experience. Was it my imagination? Was my guardian angel real or a dream?

Glancing up, I noticed my OB's partner standing at the foot of my bed. "Looks like you had quite a scare last night," she said, "But everything appears fine now."

My memory sharpened as the cobwebs cleared away. Thank you, Lord, for your great love and the guardian angel you sent to comfort me! I prayed for an opportunity to express my gratitude to Betty, but was released from the hospital before her next scheduled shift. Busy with a newborn and a preschooler, my good intentions were soon thrust to

PRAYERS FOR GOD'S PROVISION

the back of my mind.

A year rolled by, and my daughter's first birthday arrived in a flash. While replaying the night of my daughter's birth in my mind, I remembered the compassion Betty had shared on that fearful night—and my prayer for a chance to thank her one day.

Suddenly, a woman's face appeared before my mind's eye—a young mom who had visited our church the previous week. The mental images seemed to match. Could this young mom be Betty!? I wondered. A tingle ran up my spine.

The following Sunday, I watched for the new lady. From a distance, I saw her carrying one son in her arms and holding another by the hand. Recognizing her sweet smile, I introduced myself and quickly asked, "You're a nurse at the hospital, aren't you?"

"Yes," Betty replied in the same gentle voice I will always remember.

PRAYERS FOR GOD'S PROVISION

"Your prayers and compassion meant so much to me the night my daughter was born … thank you!" I said with a warm embrace.

Awestruck, I thanked my Heavenly Father, too—for answering my prayer for comfort and assurance—through Betty, my guardian angel![22]

May these words of mine, which I have prayed before the LORD, be near to the LORD our God day and night, that he may uphold the cause of his servant and the cause of his people … according to each day's need, so that all the peoples of the earth may know that the LORD is God and that there is no other.

1 KINGS 8:59–60 TLB

PRAYERS FOR GOD'S PROVISION

SIMPLY ASK!

I closed the door. I told myself it was to shut out the noise from our busy family, but maybe it was to shut out the frustration and confusion of life.

Dropping to my knees beside the bed, I groaned, "Lord, I need you! My contract is about to end. What will I do? I have bills to pay. I have eight mouths to feed!"

I searched my soul while I waited for an answer. *Do I have the wrong expectations? Do we have ongoing sin in our family? Is my attitude wrong? Show me, God, if my heart's not right.*

"Lord, we can't do this again. I know it was your will that I was laid off three years ago, and you brought us through two years without steady work, but please not again!"

Strains of "Are You Washed in the Blood of the Lamb?" penetrated my bedroom door as my sixteen-year-old son practiced his guitar. I answered the question that seemed addressed to me. "Of

PRAYERS FOR GOD'S PROVISION

course, I am!"

Looking into my heart, I searched for the answer to a different question. "Is my heart right? Is the lack of a contract a consequence for unwise decisions? Lord, forgive me for getting into debt. I should have trusted your provision. I want to pay off the debt. I'm willing to sell the house—or not sell it, just show me your will."

I sat a few moments in silence, seeking the answer. As the Lord brought issues to my mind, I confessed them to him.

I heard my two youngest children squeal with laughter. "Lord, I'm so grateful for my family and how you've always provided for us. You are so awesome, Lord. I know you'll provide for us now, but in my weakness, I'm wondering how. We need you, Lord!"

"Where's Daddy?" I heard through the door.

"He's in the bedroom," I heard my wife say. "He's having a talk with God."

"Why? What's wrong?"

PRAYERS FOR GOD'S PROVISION

"I think he's asking for a job."

Her words struck me immediately. According to the Bible, all I had to do was ask. "Yes, Lord," I said out loud. "I need work. *You* are our provision. It's not how good I am or how hard I work, it's all you. Lord, hear me, I need your answer!" In time I felt a peace—a reassurance that God's faithfulness was bigger than my problem.

I opened the door and found that life continued in the usual way. I found children sweeping floors, brushing teeth, and rinsing dishes under the direction of my wife. I called my family together and sat down to the remains of the breakfast I'd missed.

I opened my Bible and began to share between mouthfuls of eggs and toast. "I want to tell you about the time I just had with the Lord. I was feeling helpless, but I'm reassured that *he* will provide."

"Chirp, chirp, chirp." My cell phone chimed, and I jumped to answer it.

"Yes, this is Bill Rockett."

PRAYERS FOR GOD'S PROVISION

"Hello, Bill, this is Dave Banner with 'Company A.' I'd like to talk with you about an opening we have in Pasadena, California. A conversation ensued to address the job description and my qualifications.

After the conversation ended, I hurried in to tell my family.

"Well," I beamed, "that was a job possibility. It's in Southern California." I spoke with raised eyebrows, thinking about the expense of living in that part of the country. "But the pay is good, so I think we could make it."

I began to discuss the potential contract with my wife. My eggs were still half eaten when my cell phone chirped again.

"Hello, this is Bill Rockett."

"Bill, this is Jennifer Ayala with 'Company B.' I have an opening for a consultant in New Jersey. Would you be interested?"

"Yes, I'd like to hear more," I responded, and a lengthy interchange followed.

PRAYERS FOR GOD'S PROVISION

When I opened the bedroom door again, I met my wife's questioning eyes. "Another job possibility," I said. "This one's in New Jersey."

I finally managed to finish the last of my breakfast when the phone rang again! This time it was an opportunity in Virginia. Not two hours before, my future had looked bleak, but now I had three options on the table. The phone continued to chime that day with each of these three companies vying for my services, scrambling to schedule interviews and secure a contract before the others.

The Great Provider had come through. I had questioned for a time, but he had plans. He wanted to reiterate his promises to my family and me: "Your heavenly Father knows that you need all these things. But seek first His kingdom and His righteousness, and all these things will be added to you" (Matthew 6:32, 33 NASB). Today we enjoy God's blessings in Southern California in answer to that morning's prayers.[23]

Prayers for God's Provision

When my people in their need look for water, when their throats are dry with thirst, then I, the Lord, will answer their prayer; I, the God of Israel, will never abandon them.

I will make rivers flow among barren hills and springs of water run in the valleys. I will turn the desert into pools of water and the dry land into flowing springs.

People will see this and know that I, the Lord, have done it. They will come to understand that Israel's holy God has made it happen.

Isaiah 41:17–18, 20 GNT

PRAYERS FOR GOD'S PROVISION

MORE THAN ENOUGH

Soon a lot of people from the nearby villages walked around the lake to where [Jesus] was. When he saw them coming, he was overcome with pity and healed their sick.

Toward evening the disciples approached him. "We're out in the country and it's getting late. Dismiss the people so they can go to the villages and get some supper."

But Jesus said, "There is no need to dismiss them. You give them supper."

"All we have are five loaves of bread and two fish," they said.

Jesus said, "Bring them here." Then he had the people sit on the grass. He took the five loaves and two fish, lifted his face to heaven in prayer, blessed, broke, and gave the bread to the disciples. The disciples then gave the food to the congregation. They all ate their fill. They gathered twelve baskets of leftovers. About five thousand were fed.[24]

Prayers for God's Deliverance

––––– ⌘ –––––

The Mighty One, God, the Lord, *speaks....*
"Call upon me in the day of trouble;
I will deliver you, and you will honor me."

Psalm 50:1, 15

––––– ⌘ –––––

An intercessor ... is like a live wire closing
the gap between the saving power of God
and the sinful men who have been cut off
from that power.

HANNAH HURNARD

You will pray to [God], and he will hear you,
When men are brought low and you say,
"Lift them up!"
then he will save the downcast.
He will deliver even one who is not innocent,
who will be delivered through
the cleanness of your hands.

JOB 22:27, 29–30

PRAYERS FOR GOD'S DELIVERANCE

THE DAY NOAH FOUND THE LORD

As a young girl in our small, rural community, I overheard the adults talking to one another about a problem caused by a young man who lived just down the road with his wife, Lee, his son, Donald Ray, and a little daughter called Sissy. In a place as small as Hill Creek, whatever was happening in any of the households was seldom kept a secret.

It was a well-known fact that Noah was a likable man except when he was under the influence of alcohol. His addiction was not only a terrible burden for his wife and their two small children, but it was a trial for the entire community, as well. Because most of the people who lived there were strict Baptists and teetotalers, they had no idea how to handle the matter. They had little experience with alcoholism, and few had wrestled with an addiction problem. Many friends, including his sister, Mrs. Vurda, had prayed earnestly for Noah for years, seemingly without results.

PRAYERS FOR GOD'S DELIVERANCE

One year during the scheduled summer revival meeting, Noah had been persuaded to attend. As the congregation sang, "Come home, come home, ye that are weary, come home," Noah came under great conviction and made his way to the mourner's bench.

He sat surrounded by those who loved him and were praying for his salvation. He knelt with his face in his hands and cried out to the Lord. A great miracle happened that day in that little country church, and I was there to witness it. Then an equally remarkable thing happened.

Mrs. Vurda was a very quiet, calm woman, but when she saw what was happening to her brother and realized that God had answered her prayers, without warning, she stretched her arms upward and began "shouting" her thanks to God. The loud praise lasted for only a few minutes, perhaps only seconds. Mrs. Vurda was truly "caught up in the Spirit," oblivious to everything around her except that the "prodigal son" had come home. The prayers

PRAYERS FOR GOD'S DELIVERANCE

of Noah's mother had not been answered in her lifetime, but a prayerful sister saw her brother being truly born again that day.

Many years later, when Noah was an old man, I attended that same little church while I was in town visiting my parents. Noah was sitting in a corner pew near the back of the church. His face seemed to light up as he reached out and hugged me. "Oh, Rita," he said, calling me by the pet name from my childhood, "you don't know what this means to me. I'm so glad to see one of the kids I knew, now all grown and raising a family."

During the service, a song was chosen I remembered from long ago: "What a wonderful change in my life has been wrought, since Jesus came into my heart." Noah's experience of God's grace had changed his life completely. He had been delivered by the power of God through the gift of prayer.[25]

PRAYERS FOR GOD'S DELIVERANCE

He will deliver the needy who cry out,

the afflicted who have no one to help.

He will take pity on the weak and the needy

and save the needy from death.

He will rescue them from oppression

and violence.

PSALM 72:12–14

PRAYERS FOR GOD'S DELIVERANCE

A PRECIOUS GIFT

Although it was not wrapped in shiny paper or tied with a beautiful bow, Sandy gave me the best gift I have ever received. The answer God supplied through eleven persons gathered in her living room gave me back my life.

The trouble all began on November 5, 1999, when my life came to a standstill. I could not eat. I could not sleep. I could not make decisions. I certainly could not continue my daily activities and career. A doctor's visit indicated that my body's reaction to steroid medication, along with my genetic makeup, had spiraled me into a deep clinical depression. My physician prescribed some antidepressants and instructed his nurse to set up an appointment for me with a local psychiatrist.

We waited three long weeks for that appointment. I don't know who thought it was longer — my husband or me. All I wanted to do was to lie in our bedroom and stare at the ceiling. I could not laugh, and I could not cry. My bedroom became a silent

PRAYERS FOR GOD'S DELIVERANCE

prison where I barricaded myself away from the telephone, from the outside world, and even from some of my own family members.

At my initial psychiatric appointment, my new doctor noted on my record that I had the following factors in my favor: a supportive husband and family, a stable teaching career, and motivation to get better. I told her, "I will do whatever is necessary to be myself again!"

Three different medications and partial hospitalization were prescribed. For someone who wanted to feel better fast, it was not good news to learn that these medications would take two to three weeks to take effect.

Friends and family prayed for me day after day. Sandy's husband, Bill, had a friend in the mental healthcare field, and he continually shared words of encouragement from this friend with my husband. His words kept me hanging on, too, to know that clinical depression can almost always be

PRAYERS FOR GOD'S DELIVERANCE

treated if the right combination of medications can be found.

However, Sandy and Bill's son Trent was extremely concerned. There was never a time in his young life that Trent did not know me. It was he and our son, at ages four and five, who had painted a blue tempura cross on brand-new carpet in our family room. One day in January, while inquiring about my health, he said to Sandy, "Mom, we say we believe in prayer. Why don't you have a prayer meeting for Zeta?" Sandy jumped on the idea, calling Don, my husband, to seek permission to invite a few couples to pray for me and to invite us to attend. Don knew that prospects were dim for my attendance at any function, much less a prayer meeting in my behalf, but he agreed to the idea.

To this day, I have no idea why I went. The probability is great that I attended out of courtesy to this longtime friend. Sandy sat just to my left in the group, and she started the meeting by reading

PRAYERS FOR GOD'S DELIVERANCE

a Scripture. Then, very tactfully, she said that we would start praying around the group, beginning on her left and then she would conclude. This allowed everyone a chance to pray before the circle got to me. One by one, each of our closest friends and our pastor poured their hearts out to God on my behalf. More than one prayer was spiked with tears of compassion. Don was overwhelmed with gratitude for the love and support. I was still in a place where I could neither laugh nor cry, and I could not voice a prayer when it was my turn.

However, when I awoke the next morning, I was more like my "real" self than I had been since early November. My next appointment with the psychiatrist was early the next week. A still, small voice from deep within nudged me: *You are much better. You must share what I have done in your life.* When I met with the doctor, I credited the combination of medications "kicking in" on January 29, but I also told of Sandy's prayer gathering for me on

PRAYERS FOR GOD'S DELIVERANCE

the evening of January 28. The doctor's reaction? A knowing smile and a great big hug.

Much more than ever before, I read James 5:16 with confidence: "The prayer of a righteous man is powerful and effective." No, it was not wrapped in shiny paper nor tied with a beautiful bow, but my friend Sandy asked others to share in the gift that brought me back to life. It was the healing, delivering gift of prayer.[26]

PRAYERS FOR GOD'S DELIVERANCE

Every chain that spirits wear
Crumbles in the breath of prayer.

JOHN GREENLEAF WHITTIER

Deliver me from my enemies, O my God;
defend and protect me from those who rise up
against me. Deliver me from and lift me
above those who work evil and save me
from bloodthirsty men.

PSALM 59:1–2 AMP

PRAYERS FOR GOD'S DELIVERANCE

QUICK, GET UP!

It was about this time that King Herod arrested some who belonged to the church, intending to persecute them. He had James, the brother of John, put to death with the sword. When he saw that this pleased the Jews, he proceeded to seize Peter also. This happened during the Feast of Unleavened Bread. After arresting him, he put him in prison, handing him over to be guarded by four squads of four soldiers each. Herod intended to bring him out for public trial after the Passover.

So Peter was kept in prison, but the church was earnestly praying to God for him.

The night before Herod was to bring him to trial, Peter was sleeping between two soldiers, bound with two chains, and sentries stood guard at the entrance. Suddenly an angel of the Lord appeared and a light shone in the cell. He struck Peter on the side and woke him up. "Quick, get up!" he said, and the chains fell off Peter's wrists.

Then the angel said to him, "Put on your

PRAYERS FOR GOD'S DELIVERANCE

clothes and sandals." And Peter did so. "Wrap your cloak around you and follow me," the angel told him. Peter followed him out of the prison, but he had no idea that what the angel was doing was really happening; he thought he was seeing a vision. They passed the first and second guards and came to the iron gate leading to the city. It opened for them by itself, and they went through it. When they had walked the length of one street, suddenly the angel left him.

Then Peter came to himself and said, "Now I know without a doubt that the Lord sent his angel and rescued me from Herod's clutches and from everything the Jewish people were anticipating."[27]

Rise up! Come to our help, and deliver us for Your mercy's sake and because of Your steadfast love!

PSALM 44:26 AMP

PRAYERS FOR GOD'S DELIVERANCE

THE TERRIFIED JAILER

Once when we were going to the place of prayer, we were met by a slave girl who had a spirit by which she predicted the future. She earned a great deal of money for her owners by fortune-telling. This girl followed Paul and the rest of us, shouting. "These men are servants of the Most High God, who are telling you the way to be saved." She kept this up for many days. Finally Paul became so troubled that he turned around and said to the spirit. "In the name of Jesus Christ I command you to come out of her!" At that moment the spirit left her.

When the owners of the slave girl realized that their hope of making money was gone, they seized Paul and Silas and dragged them into the marketplace to face the authorities. They brought them before the magistrates and said, "These men are Jews, and are throwing our city into an uproar by advocating customs unlawful for us Romans to accept or practice."

PRAYERS FOR GOD'S DELIVERANCE

The crowd joined in the attack against Paul and Silas, and the magistrates ordered them to be stripped and beaten. After they had been severely flogged, they were thrown into prison, and the jailer was commanded to guard them carefully. Upon receiving such orders, he put them in the inner cell and fastened their feet to the stocks.

About midnight Paul and Silas were praying and singing hymns to God, and the other prisoners were listening to them. Suddenly, there was such a violent earthquake that the foundations of the prison were shaken. At once all the prison doors flew open and everybody's chains came loose. The jailer woke up, and when he saw the prison doors open, he drew his sword and was about to kill himself because he thought the prisoners had escaped. But Paul shouted, "Don't harm yourself! We are all here!"

The jailer called for lights, rushed in and fell trembling before Paul and Silas. He then brought

PRAYERS FOR GOD'S DELIVERANCE

them out and asked, "Sirs, what must I do to be saved?"

They replied, "Believe in the Lord Jesus, and you will be saved—you and your household." Then they spoke the word of the Lord to him and to all the others in his house. At that hour of the night the jailer took them and washed their wounds; then immediately he and all his family were baptized. The jailer brought them into his house and set a meal before them; he was filled with joy because he had come to believe in God—he and his family.

When it was daylight, the magistrates sent their officers to the jailer with the order: "Release those men." The jailer told Paul, "The magistrates have ordered that you and Silas be released. Now you can leave. Go in peace."[28]

NOTES

1. *Defeating the Fierce Warriors* by Andrea Garney (Tulsa, Oklahoma). Used by permission of the author.
2. *Whoosh!* by Nancy Hoag (Bozeman, Montana). Used by permission of the author.
3. *Could This Be the Something?* by Angela Epps (New Prague, Minnesota). Used by permission of the author.
4. *Mother Lecture Number Seven* by Joanne Schulte (Santa Ana, California). Used by permission of the author.
5. *All's Right with the World* by Zaphra Reskakis (New York, New York). Used by permission of the author.
6. *One Man's Prayer*, Joshua 10:1–14 TLB.
7. *The Great Physician* by Matthew Kinne (Traverse City, Michigan). Used by permission of the author.
8. *Perfect Healing* by Mary A. Hake (Crooked River Ranch, Oregon). Used by permission of the author.
9. *Hold On!* by Michelle J. Dyett-Welcome (Far Rockaway, New York). Used by permission of the author.
10. *Hope Deferred* by Jeff Adams (Kingman, Arizona). Used by permission.
11. *A Son to Hold*, 2 Kings 4:11–12, 14–21, 25–29, 31–37.
12. *A Prayer for God's Best* by Shanna D. Gregor (Amarillo, Texas). Used by permission of the author.
13. *Thank You, Lord* by Anna M. Popescu (Chino Valley, Arizona). Used by permission of the author.
14. *The Right Place for Mother* by Eileen Key (San Antonio, Texas). Used by permission of the author.
15. *In Transition* by Kimberly Strootman (Broken Arrow, Oklahoma). Used by permission of the author.
16. *Consider This Person* by Wanda Waterman St. Louis (NS, Canada). Used by permission of the author.
17. *Instructions for a Special Son*, Judges 13:2–21 TLB.
18. *235 Prayers Answered* by G. E. Dabbs (Calera, Alabama). Used by permission of the author.

NOTES

19. *Give Us This Day Our Daily Bread* by Kathryn R. Deering (Ann Arbor, Michigan). Used by permission of the author.
20. *David's Prayer for Safety*, 1 Samuel 19:9 – 13 TLB.
21. *Betty Jo Prayers* by Zeta Davidson (Kansas City, Missouri). Used by permission of the author.
22. *Guardian Angel* by Cindy L. Heflin (Dayton, Ohio). Used by permission of the author.
23. *Simply Ask!* by Carmen Rockett (Palmdale, California). Used by permission of the author.
24. *More Than Enough*, Matthew 14:13 – 21 MSG.
25. *The Day Noah Found the Lord* by Loretta Miller Mehl (Eugene, Oregon). Used by permission of the author.
26. *A Precious Gift* by Zeta Davidson (Kansas City, Missouri). Used by permission of the author.
27. *Quick, Get Up!*, Acts 12:1 – 11.
28. *The Terrified Jailer*, Acts 16:16 – 36.

Also Available:

THE GIFT
OF ANGELS

ISBN-10: 0-310-80215-6
ISBN-13: 978-0-310-80215-0

THE GIFT
OF MIRACLES

ISBN-10: 0-310-81183-X
ISBN-13: 978-0-310-81183-1

At Inspirio, we would love to
hear your stories and
your feedback.

Please send your comments to us by
way of email at
icares@zondervan.com
or to the address below:

inspirio

Attn: Inspirio Cares
5300 Patterson Avenue SE
Grand Rapids, MI 49530

If you would like further information
about Inspirio and the products
we create, please visit us at
www.inspiriogifts.com.

Thank you and God bless!